MW01274530

FRANK LLOYD WRIGHT'S
MASTERWORKS

2000 DELUXE ENGAGEMENT BOOK

WITH PHOTOGRAPHS BY PEDRO E. GUERRERO

Pomegranate

THE FRANK LLOYD WRIGHT FOUNDATION

FRANK LLOYD WRIGHT'S
MASTERWORKS

Pedro Guerrero—then a twenty-two-year-old fresh out of art school—began working for Frank Lloyd Wright (1867–1959) sixty years ago. When the beginning photographer arrived for his interview at Wright's Arizona home, Taliesin West was little more than two years old and, in fact, was still rising from the desert with the help of the Taliesin Fellowship, the architect's school of apprentices. "What are you doing now?" asked Wright. "Nothing. I'm unemployed," replied Guerrero. "Would you like to work for us? We've just lost our photographer." The young visitor was astounded: "I'd love to work for you, but as you can see I have a lot to learn." Wright said simply: "I'll teach you. The pay isn't much, but you can eat here. You can start now." □ Thus began a twenty-year relationship in which Guerrero became an apprentice himself and photographed many of Wright's new buildings as or just before they were completed, later traveling from his home in the New York area to Taliesin West as well as to Taliesin, Wright's summer home in Spring Green, Wisconsin. He photographed notable Wright houses of the period, some of Wright's most outstanding religious structures, internationally renowned landmarks such as the S. C. Johnson and Son Administration Building, and frequently even Wright. □ On the following pages a selection of Guerrero's photographs is paired with architectural drawings prepared by Wright and his office for the same buildings. Many of these are the evocative color renderings presented to clients to entice them into the excitement of Wright's vision. Always an extraordinary draftsman, Wright was about the same age as Guerrero when he visited the noted architect Louis Sullivan to apply for a job—and obtained it on the strength of his skill with a pencil. Today, at the start of a new millennium, a full century after Wright began changing the way we view architecture, his works remain powerfully new and as provocative as ever.

TALIESIN WEST (1937–59), SCOTTSDALE, ARIZONA. IN 1940 WRIGHT'S WINTER HOME NEAR THE McDOWELL RANGE WAS STILL UNDER CONSTRUCTION.

DECEMBER □ JANUARY

MONDAY 361   BOXING DAY OBSERVED (CANADA AND UK)

27

TUESDAY 362

28

WEDNESDAY 363 ◑

29

THURSDAY 364

30

FRIDAY 365

31

SATURDAY 1   NEW YEAR'S DAY

1

SUNDAY 2

2

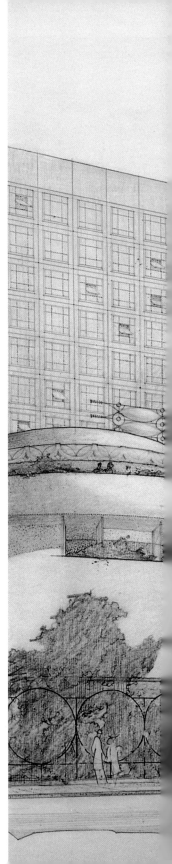

SOLOMON R. GUGGENHEIM MUSEUM (1943–59), NEW YORK CITY.
WRIGHT LIKENED THIS RENOWNED SPIRALING BUILDING TO A NAUTILUS SHELL.

JANUARY

S	S	M	T	W	T	F	S	S	M	T	W	T	F	S	S	M	T	W	T	F	S	S	M	T	W	T	F	S	S	M
1	2	3	4	5	6	7	8	9	10	11	12	13	14	15	16	17	18	19	20	21	22	23	24	25	26	27	28	29	30	31

JANUARY

MONDAY 3   BANK HOLIDAY (UK)

3

TUESDAY 4   BANK HOLIDAY (SCOTLAND ONLY)

4

WEDNESDAY 5

5

THURSDAY 6 ●

6

FRIDAY 7

7

SATURDAY 8

8

SUNDAY 9

9

TALIESIN WEST (1937–59), SCOTTSDALE, ARIZONA. A SPRITE FROM
THE DEMOLISHED MIDWAY GARDENS TOOK UP RESIDENCE IN THE DESERT.

JANUARY

S	M	T	W	T	F	S	S	M	T	W	T	F	S	S	M	T	W	T	F	S	S	M	T	W	T	F	S	S	M
1	2	3	4	5	6	7	8	9	10	11	12	13	14	15	16	17	18	19	20	21	22	23	24	25	26	27	28	29	30	31

JANUARY

10 MONDAY

10

11 TUESDAY

11

12 WEDNESDAY

12

13 THURSDAY

13

◑ 14 FRIDAY

14

MARTIN LUTHER KING JR.'S BIRTHDAY   15 SATURDAY

15

16 SUNDAY

16

JANUARY

MARTIN LUTHER KING JR. DAY

17 MONDAY

17

18 TUESDAY

18

19 WEDNESDAY

19

20 THURSDAY

20

○ 21 FRIDAY

21

22 SATURDAY

22

23 SUNDAY

23

TALIESIN WEST (1937–59), SCOTTSDALE, ARIZONA. WRIGHT USED DESERT STONES TO BLEND HIS HOME INTO THE SOUTHWESTERN LANDSCAPE.

JANUARY

S	S	M	T	W	T	F	S	S	M	T	W	T	F	S	S	M	T	W	T	F	S	S	M	T	W	T	F	S	S	M
1	2	3	4	5	6	7	8	9	10	11	12	13	14	15	16	17	18	19	20	21	22	23	24	25	26	27	28	29	30	31

JANUARY

MONDAY 24

24

TUESDAY 25

25

WEDNESDAY 26

26

THURSDAY 27

27

FRIDAY 28 ◑

28

SATURDAY 29

29

SUNDAY 30

30

TALIESIN WEST (1937–59), SCOTTSDALE, ARIZONA. SLOPING UPWARD LIKE THE MOUNTAINS, CANVAS ROOFS ALSO RECALLED THE SAILS OF SHIPS.

JANUARY

S	S	M	T	W	T	F	S	S	M	T	W	T	F	S	S	M	T	W	T	F	S	S	M	T	W	T	F	S	S	M
1	2	3	4	5	6	7	8	9	10	11	12	13	14	15	16	17	18	19	20	21	22	23	24	25	26	27	28	29	30	31

JANUARY ▫ FEBRUARY

31 MONDAY

31

32 TUESDAY

1

33 WEDNESDAY

2

34 THURSDAY

3

35 FRIDAY

4

● 36 SATURDAY

5

37 SUNDAY

6

FEBRUARY

T	W	T	F	S	S	**M**	T	W	T	F	S	S	**M**	T	W	T	F	S	S	**M**	T	W	T	F	S	S	**M**	T
1	2	3	4	5	6	7	8	9	10	11	12	13	14	15	16	17	18	19	20	21	22	23	24	25	26	27	28	29

FEBRUARY

MONDAY 38

7

TUESDAY 39

8

WEDNESDAY 40

9

THURSDAY 41

10

FRIDAY 42

11

SATURDAY 43 ◗   LINCOLN'S BIRTHDAY

12

SUNDAY 44

13

SUSAN LAWRENCE DANA HOUSE (1902–4), SPRINGFIELD, ILLINOIS.
ARCHES ARE USED AS A LEITMOTIF THROUGHOUT THIS PRAIRIE HOUSE.

FEBRUARY

T	W	T	F	S	S	**M**	T	W	T	F	S	S	**M**	T	W	T	F	S	S	**M**	T	W	T	F	S	S	**M**	T
1	2	3	4	5	6	7	8	9	10	11	12	13	14	15	16	17	18	19	20	21	22	23	24	25	26	27	28	29

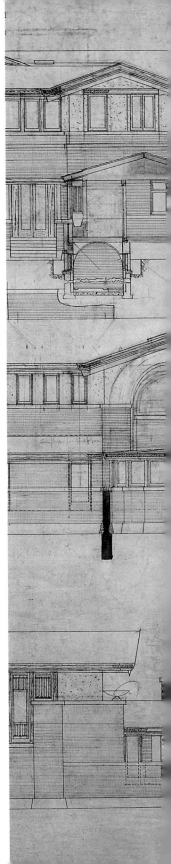

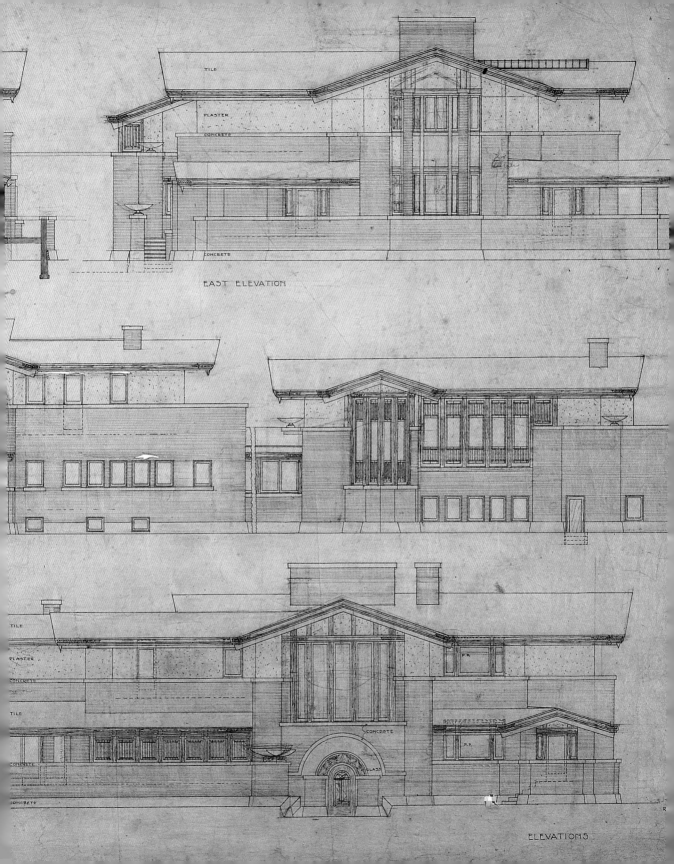

TILE

PLASTER

CONCRETE

CONCRETE

EAST ELEVATION

TILE

PLASTER

CONCRETE

TILE

CONCRETE

CONCRETE

CONCRETE

GLASS

P. P.

P. P.

ELEVATIONS

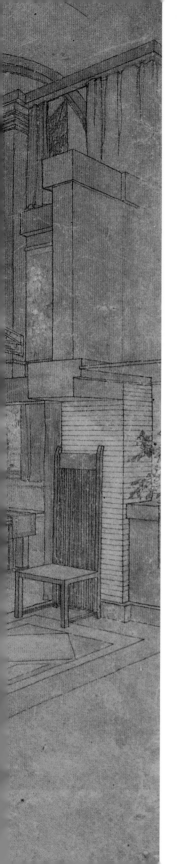

VALENTINE'S DAY

45 MONDAY

14

46 TUESDAY

15

47 WEDNESDAY

16

48 THURSDAY

17

49 FRIDAY

18

○ 50 SATURDAY

19

51 SUNDAY

20

SUSAN LAWRENCE DANA HOUSE (1902–4), SPRINGFIELD, ILLINOIS.
THE VAULTED DINING ROOM IS DRESSED IN THE WARM COLORS OF AUTUMN.

FEBRUARY

T	W	T	F	S	S	M	T	W	T	F	S	S	M	T	W	T	F	S	S	M	T	W	T	F	S	S	M	T
1	2	3	4	5	6	7	8	9	10	11	12	13	14	15	16	17	18	19	20	21	22	23	24	25	26	27	28	29

FEBRUARY

MONDAY 52   PRESIDENTS' DAY

21

TUESDAY 53   WASHINGTON'S BIRTHDAY

22

WEDNESDAY 54

23

THURSDAY 55

24

FRIDAY 56

25

SATURDAY 57

26

SUNDAY 58 ◑

27

SUSAN LAWRENCE DANA HOUSE (1902–4), SPRINGFIELD, ILLINOIS.
A SUMAC MURAL RINGING THE DINING ROOM BRINGS NATURE INDOORS.

FEBRUARY

T	W	T	F	S	S	M	T	W	T	F	S	S	M	T	W	T	F	S	S	M	T	W	T	F	S	S	M	T
1	2	3	4	5	6	7	8	9	10	11	12	13	14	15	16	17	18	19	20	21	22	23	24	25	26	27	28	29

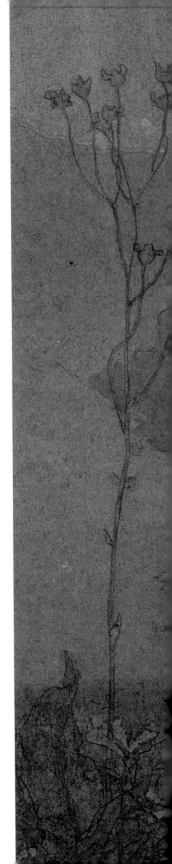

59 MONDAY

28

60 TUESDAY

29

61 WEDNESDAY

1

62 THURSDAY

2

63 FRIDAY

3

64 SATURDAY

4

65 SUNDAY

5

MARCH

W	T	F	S	S	M	T	W	T	F	S	S	M	T	W	T	F	S	S	M	T	W	T	F	S	S	M	T	W	T	F
1	2	3	4	5	6	7	8	9	10	11	12	13	14	15	16	17	18	19	20	21	22	23	24	25	26	27	28	29	30	31

● 66 MONDAY

6

67 TUESDAY

7

ASH WEDNESDAY   68 WEDNESDAY

69 THURSDAY

9

70 FRIDAY

10

71 SATURDAY

11

72 SUNDAY

12

SUSAN LAWRENCE DANA HOUSE (1902–4), SPRINGFIELD, ILLINOIS.
THE GALLERY'S TALL CEILING DWARFS TWO OF WRIGHT'S PRINT TABLES.

MARCH

W	T	F	S	S	**M**	T	W	T	F	S	S	**M**	T	W	T	F	S	S	**M**	T	W	T	F	S	S	**M**	T	W	T	F
1	2	3	4	5	6	7	8	9	10	11	12	13	14	15	16	17	18	19	20	21	22	23	24	25	26	27	28	29	30	31

MARCH

MONDAY 73

13

TUESDAY 74

14

WEDNESDAY 75

15

THURSDAY 76

16

FRIDAY 77   ST. PATRICK'S DAY ▫ BANK HOLIDAY (N. IRELAND)

17

SATURDAY 78

18

SUNDAY 79

19

SUSAN LAWRENCE DANA HOUSE (1902–4), SPRINGFIELD, ILLINOIS.
ABSTRACTED SUMAC PATTERNS ENLIVEN ART-GLASS DOORS AND WINDOWS.

MARCH

W	T	F	S	S	M	T	W	T	F	S	S	M	T	W	T	F	S	S	M	T	W	T	F	S	S	M	T	W	T	F
1	2	3	4	5	6	7	8	9	10	11	12	13	14	15	16	17	18	19	20	21	22	23	24	25	26	27	28	29	30	31

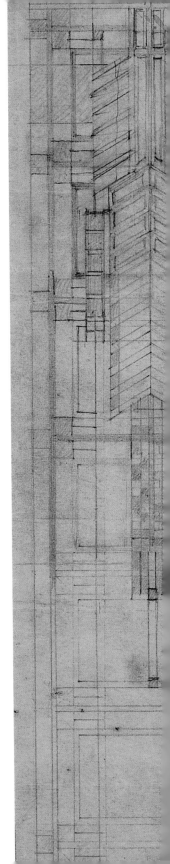

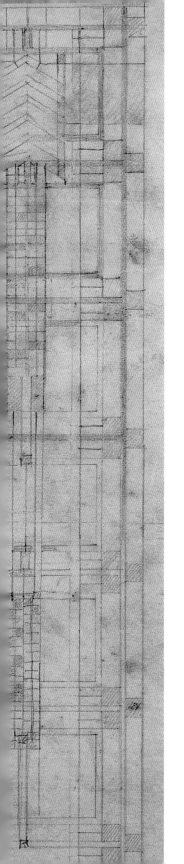

MARCH

VERNAL EQUINOX 7:35 A.M. (GMT)

○ 80 MONDAY

20

81 TUESDAY

21

82 WEDNESDAY

22

83 THURSDAY

23

84 FRIDAY

24

85 SATURDAY

25

86 SUNDAY

26

MARCH

W	T	F	S	S	**M**	T	W	T	F	S	S	**M**	T	W	T	F	S	S	**M**	T	W	T	F	S	S	**M**	T	W	T	F
1	2	3	4	5	6	7	8	9	10	11	12	13	14	15	16	17	18	19	20	21	22	23	24	25	26	27	28	29	30	31

MARCH □ APRIL

MONDAY 87

27

TUESDAY 88 ◐

28

WEDNESDAY 89

29

THURSDAY 90

30

FRIDAY 91

31

SATURDAY 92

1

SUNDAY 93   DAYLIGHT SAVING TIME BEGINS

2

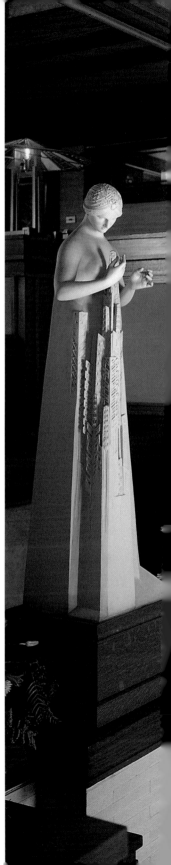

SUSAN LAWRENCE DANA HOUSE (1902–4), SPRINGFIELD, ILLINOIS.
A PENSIVE SCULPTURE BY RICHARD BOCK GREETS VISITORS AT THE ENTRY.

MARCH

W	T	F	S	S	**M**	T	W	T	F	S	S	**M**	T	W	T	F	S	S	**M**	T	W	T	F	S	S	**M**	T	W	T	F
1	2	3	4	5	6	7	8	9	10	11	12	13	14	15	16	17	18	19	20	21	22	23	24	25	26	27	28	29	30	31

APRIL

94 MONDAY

3

 95 TUESDAY

4

96 WEDNESDAY

5

97 THURSDAY

6

98 FRIDAY

7

99 SATURDAY

8

100 SUNDAY

9

APRIL

S S **M** T W T F S S **M** T W T F S S **M** T W T F S S **M** T W T F S S
1 2 3 4 5 6 7 8 9 10 11 12 13 14 15 16 17 18 19 20 21 22 23 24 25 26 27 28 29 30

APRIL

10

11

12

13

14

15

16

UNITARIAN MEETING HOUSE (1945–51), SHOREWOOD HILLS, WISCONSIN. WRIGHT CHOSE A SOARING ROOF INSTEAD OF A CHURCH STEEPLE.

APRIL

S	M	T	W	T	F	S	S	M	T	W	T	F	S	S	M	T	W	T	F	S	S	M	T	W	T	F	S	S
	1	2	3	4	5	6	7	8	9	10	11	12	13	14	15	16	17	18	19	20	21	22	23	24	25	26	27	28	29	30

APRIL

MONDAY 108

17

TUESDAY 109 ○

18

WEDNESDAY 110   PASSOVER (BEGINS AT SUNSET)

19

THURSDAY 111

20

FRIDAY 112   GOOD FRIDAY

21

SATURDAY 113   EARTH DAY

22

SUNDAY 114   EASTER SUNDAY

23

"TODAY" SHOW DEMONSTRATION (1953). WRIGHT'S HANDS ILLUSTRATED
THE UNITARIAN MEETING HOUSE AND RULES OF "ORGANIC ARCHITECTURE."

APRIL

S	M	T	W	T	F	S	S	M	T	W	T	F	S	S	M	T	W	T	F	S	S	M	T	W	T	F	S	S	M
1	2	3	4	5	6	7	8	9	10	11	12	13	14	15	16	17	18	19	20	21	22	23	24	25	26	27	28	29	30

APRIL

EASTER MONDAY (CANADA AND UK)

115 MONDAY

24

116 TUESDAY

25

◑ 117 WEDNESDAY

26

118 THURSDAY

27

119 FRIDAY

28

120 SATURDAY

29

121 SUNDAY

30

"TODAY" SHOW DEMONSTRATION (1953). WRIGHT ALSO SHOWED CON-VENTIONAL POST-AND-BEAM CONSTRUCTION METHODS THAT HE ABANDONED.

APRIL

S	S	M	T	W	T	F	S	S	M	T	W	T	F	S	S	M	T	W	T	F	S	S	M	T	W	T	F	S	S
1	2	3	4	5	6	7	8	9	10	11	12	13	14	15	16	17	18	19	20	21	22	23	24	25	26	27	28	29	30

MAY

MONDAY 122   BANK HOLIDAY (UK)

1

TUESDAY 123

2

WEDNESDAY 124

3

THURSDAY 125 ●

4

FRIDAY 126   CINCO DE MAYO

5

SATURDAY 127

6

SUNDAY 128

7

MAXIMILIAN HOFFMAN HOUSE (1955), RYE, NEW YORK. AFTER THE
CLIENT REJECTED THIS BOLD RUG DESIGN, IT WAS LATER MADE FOR TALIESIN.

MAY

M	T	W	T	F	S	S	M	T	W	T	F	S	S	M	T	W	T	F	S	S	M	T	W	T	F	S	S	M	T	W
1	2	3	4	5	6	7	8	9	10	11	12	13	14	15	16	17	18	19	20	21	22	23	24	25	26	27	28	29	30	31

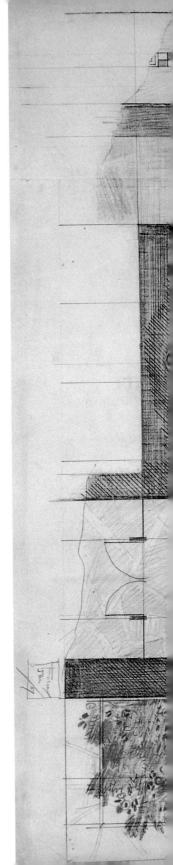

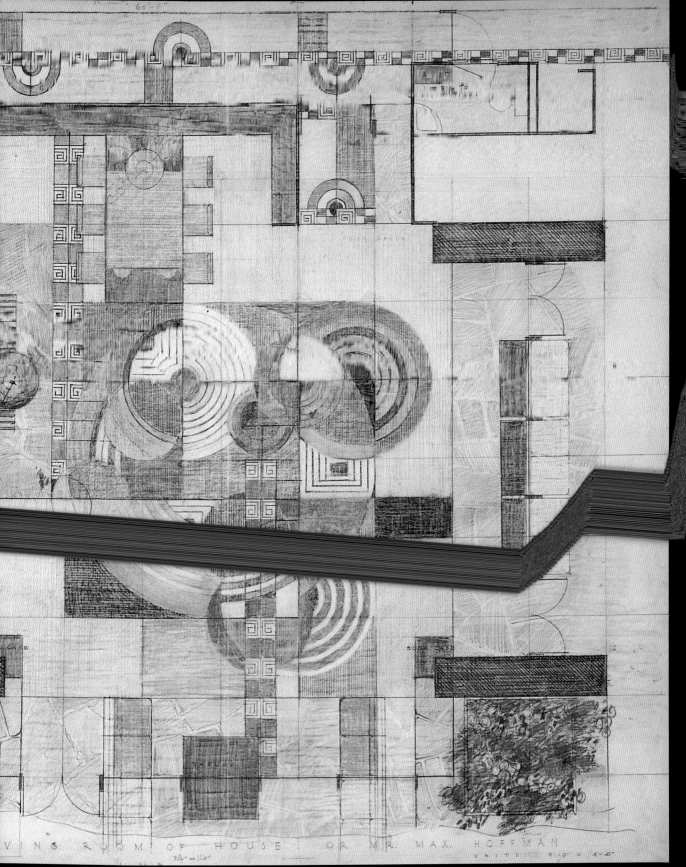

LIVING ROOM OF HOUSE OR MR MAX HOFFMAN

3/4" = 1'0"

UNITS 6'-0" X 4'-0"

MAY

8

TUESDAY 130

9

WEDNESDAY 131 ☽

10

THURSDAY 132

11

FRIDAY 133

12

SATURDAY 134

13

SUNDAY 135   MOTHER'S DAY

14

MAXIMILIAN HOFFMAN HOUSE (1955), RYE, NEW YORK. BUILT WITH
RUSTIC GRANITE WALLS, THE HOUSE LOOKS OUT OVER LONG ISLAND SOUND.

MAY

M	T	W	T	F	S	S	M	T	W	T	F	S	S	M	T	W	T	F	S	S	M	T	W	T	F	S	S	M	T	W
1	2	3	4	5	6	7	8	9	10	11	12	13	14	15	16	17	18	19	20	21	22	23	24	25	26	27	28	29	30	31

MAY

136 MONDAY

15

137 TUESDAY

16

138 WEDNESDAY

17

○ 139 THURSDAY

18

140 FRIDAY

19

ARMED FORCES DAY

20

142 SUNDAY

21

MAY

M T W T F S S M T W T F S S M T W T F S S M T W T F S S M T W
1 2 3 4 5 6 7 8 9 10 11 12 13 14 15 16 17 18 19 20 21 22 23 24 25 26 27 28 29 30 31

MAY

VICTORIA DAY (CANADA)

143 MONDAY

22

144 TUESDAY

23

145 WEDNESDAY

24

146 THURSDAY

25

◗ 147 FRIDAY

26

148 SATURDAY

27

149 SUNDAY

28

TALIESIN III (1925–59), SPRING GREEN, WISCONSIN. WRIGHT'S SERENE DINING ALCOVE IS TUCKED INTO A CORNER OF THE LIVING ROOM.

MAY

M	T	W	T	F	S	S	M	T	W	T	F	S	S	M	T	W	T	F	S	S	M	T	W	T	F	S	S	M	T	W
1	2	3	4	5	6	7	8	9	10	11	12	13	14	15	16	17	18	19	20	21	22	23	24	25	26	27	28	29	30	31

MAY ▢ JUNE

MONDAY 150   MEMORIAL DAY OBSERVED ▢ LATE BANK HOLIDAY (UK)

29

TUESDAY 151   MEMORIAL DAY

30

WEDNESDAY 152

31

THURSDAY 153

1

FRIDAY 154 ●

2

SATURDAY 155

3

SUNDAY 156

4

ROMEO AND JULIET WINDMILL (1896), SPRING GREEN, WISCONSIN. ONE OF WRIGHT'S EARLIEST STRUCTURES SERVED HIS AUNTS' HILLSIDE HOME SCHOOL.

MAY

M	T	W	T	F	S	S	M	T	W	T	F	S	S	M	T	W	T	F	S	S	M	T	W	T	F	S	S	M	T	W
1	2	3	4	5	6	7	8	9	10	11	12	13	14	15	16	17	18	19	20	21	22	23	24	25	26	27	28	29	30	31

JUNE

5

158 TUESDAY

6

159 WEDNESDAY

7

FRANK LLOYD WRIGHT'S BIRTHDAY   160 THURSDAY

8

 161 FRIDAY

9

162 SATURDAY

10

163 SUNDAY

11

						JUNE																							
T	F	S	S	**M**	T	W	T	F	S	S	**M**	T	W	T	F	S	S	**M**	T	W	T	F	S	S	**M**	T	W	T	F
1	2	3	4	5	6	7	8	9	10	11	12	13	14	15	16	17	18	19	20	21	22	23	24	25	26	27	28	29	30

JUNE

12

13

FLAG DAY

14

15

○ 168 FRIDAY

16

17

FATHER'S DAY

18

TALIESIN FELLOWSHIP COMPLEX (1932), SPRING GREEN, WISCONSIN.
SCORES OF APPRENTICES LEARNED HERE UNDER WRIGHT'S PRACTICED HAND.

JUNE

T	F	S	S	M	T	W	T	F	S	S	M	T	W	T	F	S	S	M	T	W	T	F	S	S	M	T	W	T	F
1	2	3	4	5	6	7	8	9	10	11	12	13	14	15	16	17	18	19	20	21	22	23	24	25	26	27	28	29	30

JUNE

MONDAY 171

19

TUESDAY 172

2o

WEDNESDAY 173   SUMMER SOLSTICE 1:48 A.M. (GMT)

21

THURSDAY 174

22

FRIDAY 175

23

SATURDAY 176

24

SUNDAY 177 ◑

25

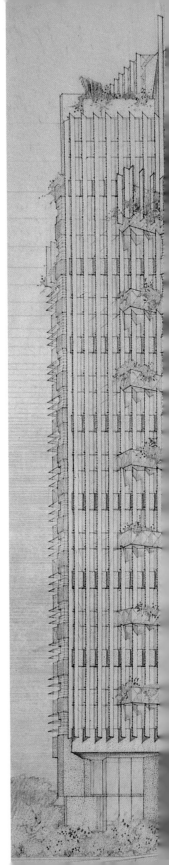

H. C. PRICE COMPANY TOWER (1952–56), BARTLESVILLE, OKLAHOMA.
FOR HIS ONLY SKYSCRAPER, WRIGHT REVIVED A 1929 DESIGN FOR NEW YORK.

JUNE

T	F	S	S	M	T	W	T	F	S	S	M	T	W	T	F	S	S	M	T	W	T	F	S	S	M	T	W	T	F
1	2	3	4	5	6	7	8	9	10	11	12	13	14	15	16	17	18	19	20	21	22	23	24	25	26	27	28	29	30

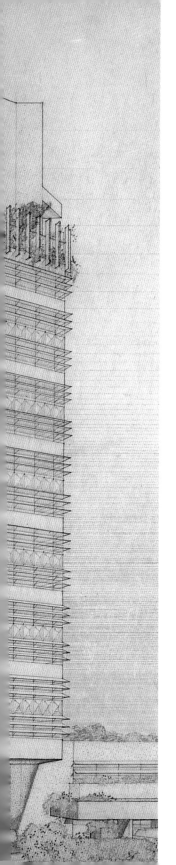

JUNE  JULY

178 MONDAY
26

179 TUESDAY
27

180 WEDNESDAY
28

181 THURSDAY
29

182 FRIDAY
30

CANADA DAY (CANADA)   ● 183 SATURDAY
1

184 SUNDAY
2

JULY

S S M T W T F S S M T W T F S S M T W T F S S M T W T F S S M
1 2 3 4 5 6 7 8 9 10 11 12 13 14 15 16 17 18 19 20 21 22 23 24 25 26 27 28 29 30 31

JULY

CANADA DAY OBSERVED (CANADA)   185 MONDAY

3

INDEPENDENCE DAY   186 TUESDAY

4

---

187 WEDNESDAY

5

---

188 THURSDAY

6

---

189 FRIDAY

7

---

 190 SATURDAY

8

---

191 SUNDAY

9

"SIXTY YEARS OF LIVING ARCHITECTURE" EXHIBITION (1953). THE ARCHITECT POSED AT HIS RETROSPECTIVE WITH A MODEL OF THE PRICE TOWER.

JULY

S	S	**M**	T	W	T	F	S	S	**M**	T	W	T	F	S	S	**M**	T	W	T	F	S	S	**M**	T	W	T	F	S	S	**M**
1	2	3	4	5	6	7	8	9	10	11	12	13	14	15	16	17	18	19	20	21	22	23	24	25	26	27	28	29	30	31

JULY

MONDAY 192

10

TUESDAY 193

11

WEDNESDAY 194   BANK HOLIDAY (N. IRELAND)

12

THURSDAY 195

13

FRIDAY 196

14

SATURDAY 197

15

SUNDAY 198 ○

16

SAN FRANCISCO CALL BUILDING (PROJECT) (c. 1913), SAN FRANCISCO.
WRIGHT'S REINFORCED-CONCRETE SKYSCRAPER WAS NEVER BUILT.

JULY
S S M T W T F S S M T W T F S S M T W T F S S M T W T F S S M
1 2 3 4 5 6 7 8 9 10 11 12 13 14 15 16 17 18 19 20 21 22 23 24 25 26 27 28 29 30 31

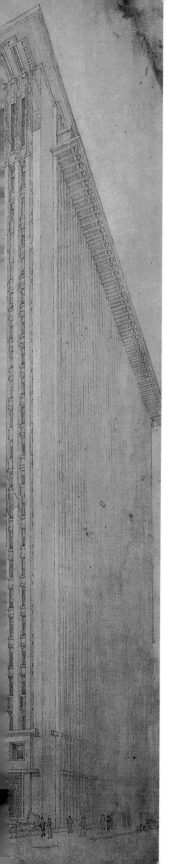

199 MONDAY

17

200 TUESDAY

18

201 WEDNESDAY

19

202 THURSDAY

2o

203 FRIDAY

21

204 SATURDAY

22

205 SUNDAY

23

JULY

S S M T W T F S S M T W T F S S M T W T F S S M T W T F S S M
1 2 3 4 5 6 7 8 9 10 11 12 13 14 15 16 17 18 19 20 21 22 23 24 25 26 27 28 29 30 31

JULY

MONDAY 206 ◑

24

TUESDAY 207

25

WEDNESDAY 208

26

THURSDAY 209

27

FRIDAY 210

28

SATURDAY 211

29

SUNDAY 212

30

SAN FRANCISCO CALL BUILDING (PROJECT) (c. 1913), SAN FRANCISCO.
A MODEL STOOD FOR YEARS IN WRIGHT'S STUDIO AT TALIESIN.

JULY

S	M	T	W	T	F	S	S	M	T	W	T	F	S	S	M	T	W	T	F	S	S	M	T	W	T	F	S	S	M	T
1	2	3	4	5	6	7	8	9	10	11	12	13	14	15	16	17	18	19	20	21	22	23	24	25	26	27	28	29	30	31

JULY □ AUGUST

● 213 MONDAY

31

214 TUESDAY

1

215 WEDNESDAY

2

216 THURSDAY

3

217 FRIDAY

4

218 SATURDAY

5

219 SUNDAY

6

AUGUST

T	W	T	F	S	S	**M**	T	W	T	F	S	S	**M**	T	W	T	F	S	S	**M**	T	W	T	F	S	S	**M**	T	W	T
1	2	3	4	5	6	7	8	9	10	11	12	13	14	15	16	17	18	19	20	21	22	23	24	25	26	27	28	29	30	31

AUGUST

MONDAY 220   BANK HOLIDAY (SCOTLAND)

7

TUESDAY 221

8

WEDNESDAY 222

9

THURSDAY 223

10

FRIDAY 224

11

SATURDAY 225

12

SUNDAY 226

13

JOHN L. RAYWARD HOUSE (1955), NEW CANAAN, CONNECTICUT.
HOUSE AND SITE MELD TOGETHER LIKE FALLINGWATER OVER ITS WATERFALL.

AUGUST

T	W	T	F	S	S	M	T	W	T	F	S	S	M	T	W	T	F	S	S	M	T	W	T	F	S	S	M	T	W	T
1	2	3	4	5	6	7	8	9	10	11	12	13	14	15	16	17	18	19	20	21	22	23	24	25	26	27	28	29	30	31

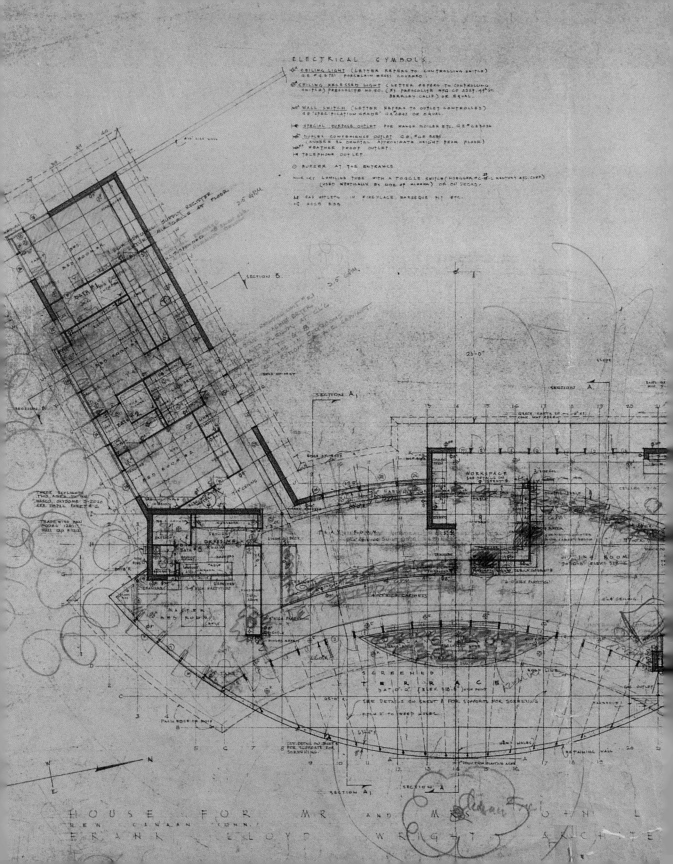

ELECTRICAL SYMBOLS.

HOUSE FOR MR AND MRS JOHN L

NEW CANAAN CONN.

FRANK LLOYD WRIGHT ARCHITECT

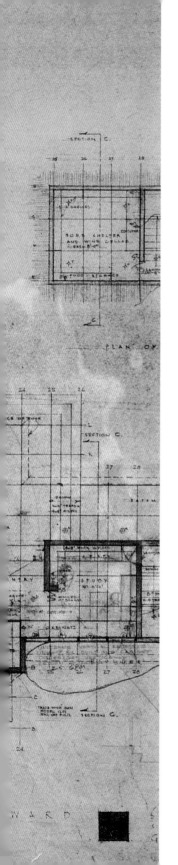

227 MONDAY

14

○ 228 TUESDAY

15

229 WEDNESDAY

16

230 THURSDAY

17

231 FRIDAY

18

232 SATURDAY

19

233 SUNDAY

20

JOHN L. RAYWARD HOUSE (1955), NEW CANAAN, CONNECTICUT.
IN THE ELLIPTICAL DESIGN, A TERRACE OVERLOOKS THE POOL AND THE POND.

AUGUST

T	W	T	F	S	S	M	T	W	T	F	S	S	M	T	W	T	F	S	S	M	T	W	T	F	S	S	M	T	W	T
1	2	3	4	5	6	7	8	9	10	11	12	13	14	15	16	17	18	19	20	21	22	23	24	25	26	27	28	29	30	31

AUGUST

MONDAY 234

21

TUESDAY 235 ◗

22

WEDNESDAY 236

23

THURSDAY 237

24

FRIDAY 238

25

SATURDAY 239

26

SUNDAY 240

27

JOHN L. RAYWARD HOUSE (1955), NEW CANAAN, CONNECTICUT.
WINDOWS ALONGSIDE THE TERRACE CURVE TO CATCH THE SUN'S RAYS.

AUGUST

T	W	T	F	S	S	M	T	W	T	F	S	S	M	T	W	T	F	S	S	M	T	W	T	F	S	S	M	T	W	T
1	2	3	4	5	6	7	8	9	10	11	12	13	14	15	16	17	18	19	20	21	22	23	24	25	26	27	28	29	30	31

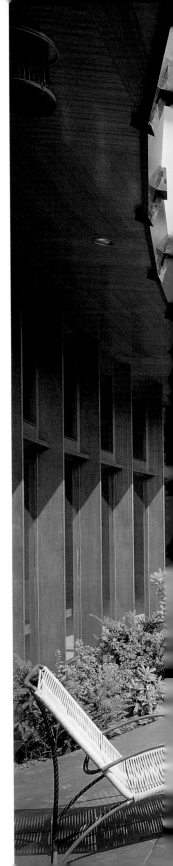

BANK HOLIDAY (UK)

241 MONDAY

28

● 242 TUESDAY

29

243 WEDNESDAY

30

244 THURSDAY

31

245 FRIDAY

1

246 SATURDAY

2

247 SUNDAY

3

SEPTEMBER

F	S	S	M	T	W	T	F	S	S	M	T	W	T	F	S	S	M	T	W	T	F	S	S	M	T	W	T	F	S
1	2	3	4	5	6	7	8	9	10	11	12	13	14	15	16	17	18	19	20	21	22	23	24	25	26	27	28	29	30

SEPTEMBER

MONDAY 248 · LABOR DAY (US AND CANADA)

4

TUESDAY 249

5

WEDNESDAY 250

6

THURSDAY 251

7

FRIDAY 252

8

SATURDAY 253

9

SUNDAY 254

10

TALIESIN FELLOWSHIP COMPLEX (1932), SPRING GREEN, WISCONSIN. WRIGHT REDESIGNED THE HILLSIDE DINING ROOM AFTER A FIRE IN 1952.

SEPTEMBER

F	S	S	M	T	W	T	F	S	S	M	T	W	T	F	S	S	M	T	W	T	F	S	S	M	T	W	T	F	S
1	2	3	4	5	6	7	8	9	10	11	12	13	14	15	16	17	18	19	20	21	22	23	24	25	26	27	28	29	30

SEPTEMBER

255 MONDAY

11

256 TUESDAY

12

○ 257 WEDNESDAY

13

258 THURSDAY

14

259 FRIDAY

15

260 SATURDAY

16

261 SUNDAY

17

SEPTEMBER

F	S	S	M	T	W	T	F	S	S	M	T	W	T	F	S	S	M	T	W	T	F	S	S	M	T	W	T	F	S
1	2	3	4	5	6	7	8	9	10	11	12	13	14	15	16	17	18	19	20	21	22	23	24	25	26	27	28	29	30

SEPTEMBER

MONDAY 262

18

TUESDAY 263

19

WEDNESDAY 264

20

THURSDAY 265 ◖

21

FRIDAY 266   AUTUMNAL EQUINOX 5:27 P.M. (GMT)

22

SATURDAY 267

23

SUNDAY 268

24

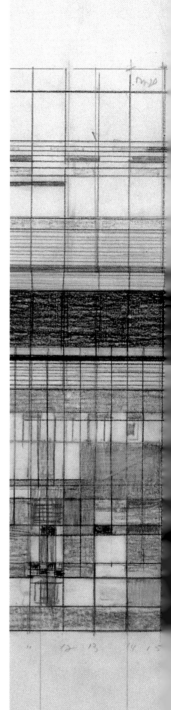

TALIESIN FELLOWSHIP COMPLEX (1932), SPRING GREEN, WISCONSIN.
THE THEATER CURTAIN IS AN ABSTRACTION OF TALIESIN IN ITS LANDSCAPE.

SEPTEMBER

F	S	S	**M**	T	W	T	F	S	S	**M**	T	W	T	F	S	S	**M**	T	W	T	F	S	S	**M**	T	W	T	F	S
1	2	3	4	5	6	7	8	9	10	11	12	13	14	15	16	17	18	19	20	21	22	23	24	25	26	27	28	29	30

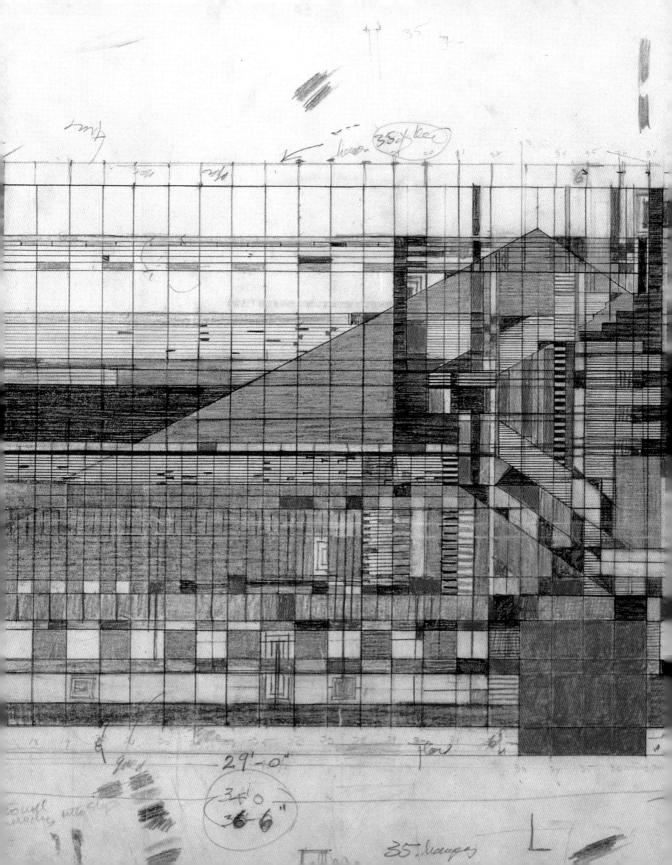

SEPTEMBER □ OCTOBER

MONDAY 269

25

TUESDAY 270

26

WEDNESDAY 271 ●

27

THURSDAY 272

28

FRIDAY 273   ROSH HASHANAH (BEGINS AT SUNSET)

29

SATURDAY 274

3o

SUNDAY 275

1

BETH SHOLOM SYNAGOGUE (1953–59), ELKINS PARK, PENNSYLVANIA.
THE MAIN SANCTUARY'S CHANDELIER SHOWERS COLOR ON THE CONGREGANTS.

SEPTEMBER

F	S	S	**M**	T	W	T	F	S	S	**M**	T	W	T	F	S	S	**M**	T	W	T	F	S	S	**M**	T	W	T	F	S
1	2	3	4	5	6	7	8	9	10	11	12	13	14	15	16	17	18	19	20	21	22	23	24	25	26	27	28	29	30

OCTOBER

276 MONDAY

2

277 TUESDAY

3

278 WEDNESDAY

4

 279 THURSDAY

5

280 FRIDAY

6

281 SATURDAY

7

YOM KIPPUR (BEGINS AT SUNSET)   282 SUNDAY

8

OCTOBER

S	M	T	W	T	F	S	S	M	T	W	T	F	S	S	M	T	W	T	F	S	S	M	T	W	T	F	S	S	M	T
1	2	3	4	5	6	7	8	9	10	11	12	13	14	15	16	17	18	19	20	21	22	23	24	25	26	27	28	29	30	31

OCTOBER

9

284 TUESDAY

10

285 WEDNESDAY

11

COLUMBUS DAY   286 THURSDAY

12

○ 287 FRIDAY

13

288 SATURDAY

14

289 SUNDAY

15

BETH SHOLOM SYNAGOGUE (1953–59), ELKINS PARK, PENNSYLVANIA.
A MOUNT SINAI IN GLASS, THE TRIANGULAR BUILDING RISES ON A STEEL FRAME.

OCTOBER

S	M	T	W	T	F	S	S	M	T	W	T	F	S	S	M	T	W	T	F	S	S	M	T	W	T	F	S	S	M	T
1	2	3	4	5	6	7	8	9	10	11	12	13	14	15	16	17	18	19	20	21	22	23	24	25	26	27	28	29	30	31

OCTOBER

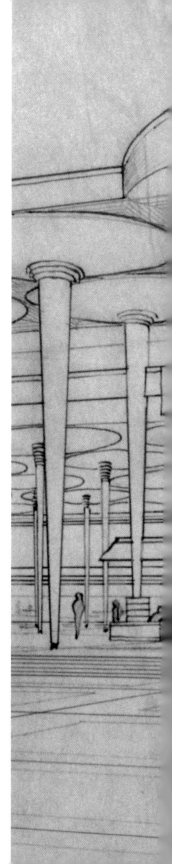

MONDAY 290

16

TUESDAY 291

17

WEDNESDAY 292

18

THURSDAY 293

19

FRIDAY 294 ◗

2o

SATURDAY 295

21

SUNDAY 296

22

S. C. JOHNSON AND SON, INC. ADMINISTRATION BUILDING (1936–39), RACINE, WISCONSIN. THE GREAT WORKROOM IS A FOREST OF COLUMNS.

OCTOBER

S	M	T	W	T	F	S	S	M	T	W	T	F	S	S	M	T	W	T	F	S	S	M	T	W	T	F	S	S	M	T
1	2	3	4	5	6	7	8	9	10	11	12	13	14	15	16	17	18	19	20	21	22	23	24	25	26	27	28	29	30	31

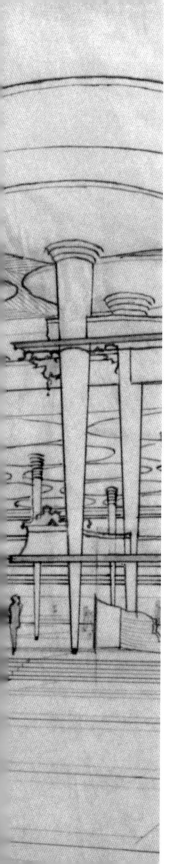

OCTOBER

297 MONDAY

23

UNITED NATIONS DAY

298 TUESDAY

24

299 WEDNESDAY

25

300 THURSDAY

26

● 301 FRIDAY

27

302 SATURDAY

28

DAYLIGHT SAVING TIME ENDS

303 SUNDAY

29

OCTOBER

S M T W T F S S M T W T F S S M T W T F S S M T W T F S S M T
1 2 3 4 5 6 7 8 9 10 11 12 13 14 15 16 17 18 19 20 21 22 23 24 25 26 27 28 29 30 31

OCTOBER □ NOVEMBER

MONDAY 304

30

TUESDAY 305   HALLOWEEN

31

WEDNESDAY 306

1

THURSDAY 307

2

FRIDAY 308

3

SATURDAY 309 ◖

4

SUNDAY 310

5

**S. C. JOHNSON AND SON, INC. ADMINISTRATION BUILDING (1936–39),
RACINE, WISCONSIN.** WRIGHT DESIGNED EVERYTHING, EVEN THE CHAIRS.

OCTOBER
S M T W T F S S M T W T F S S M T W T F S S M T W T F S S M T
1 2 3 4 5 6 7 8 9 10 11 12 13 14 15 16 17 18 19 20 21 22 23 24 25 26 27 28 29 30 31

NOVEMBER

311 MONDAY

6

ELECTION DAY

312 TUESDAY

7

313 WEDNESDAY

8

314 THURSDAY

9

VETERANS DAY OBSERVED

315 FRIDAY

10

VETERANS DAY □ REMEMBRANCE DAY (CANADA) ○ 316 SATURDAY

11

317 SUNDAY

12

NOVEMBER

W T F S S **M** T W T F S S **M** T W T F S S **M** T W T F S S **M** T W T
1 2 3 4 5 6 7 8 9 10 11 12 13 14 15 16 17 18 19 20 21 22 23 24 25 26 27 28 29 30

NOVEMBER

MONDAY 318   REMEMBRANCE DAY OBSERVED (CANADA)

13

TUESDAY 319

14

WEDNESDAY 320

15

THURSDAY 321

16

FRIDAY 322

17

SATURDAY 323

18

SUNDAY 324

19

**ANNUNCIATION GREEK ORTHODOX CHURCH (1955–61), WAUWATOSA, WIS-
CONSIN.** ORTHODOX CROSSES AND CIRCLES FILL THE INTERIOR OF THE CHURCH.

NOVEMBER
W	T	F	S	S	M	T	W	T	F	S	S	M	T	W	T	F	S	S	M	T	W	T	F	S	S	M	T	W	T
1	2	3	4	5	6	7	8	9	10	11	12	13	14	15	16	17	18	19	20	21	22	23	24	25	26	27	28	29	30

NOVEMBER

325 MONDAY

2o

326 TUESDAY

21

327 WEDNESDAY

22

THANKSGIVING DAY   328 THURSDAY

23

329 FRIDAY

24

● 330 SATURDAY

25

331 SUNDAY

26

ANNUNCIATION GREEK ORTHODOX CHURCH (1955–61), WAUWATOSA, WISCONSIN. WRIGHT BASED HIS PLAN ON THE SHAPE OF THE GREEK CROSS.

NOVEMBER

W	T	F	S	S	**M**	T	W	T	F	S	S	**M**	T	W	T	F	S	S	**M**	T	W	T	F	S	S	**M**	T	W	T
1	2	3	4	5	6	7	8	9	10	11	12	13	14	15	16	17	18	19	20	21	22	23	24	25	26	27	28	29	30

NOVEMBER □ DECEMBER

MONDAY 332

27

TUESDAY 333

28

WEDNESDAY 334

29

THURSDAY 335

30

FRIDAY 336

1

SATURDAY 337

2

SUNDAY 338

3

ANNUNCIATION GREEK ORTHODOX CHURCH (1955–61), WAUWATOSA, WISCONSIN. A DISC ROOF OF BYZANTINE BLUE SHELTERS THE BUILDING.

NOVEMBER

W	T	F	S	S	**M**	T	W	T	F	S	S	**M**	T	W	T	F	S	S	**M**	T	W	T	F	S	S	**M**	T	W	T
1	2	3	4	5	6	7	8	9	10	11	12	13	14	15	16	17	18	19	20	21	22	23	24	25	26	27	28	29	30

DECEMBER

 339 MONDAY

4

340 TUESDAY

5

341 WEDNESDAY

6

342 THURSDAY

7

343 FRIDAY

8

344 SATURDAY

9

345 SUNDAY

10

DECEMBER

F S S **M** T W T F S S **M** T W T F S S **M** T W T F S S **M** T W T F S S
1 2 3 4 5 6 7 8 9 10 11 12 13 14 15 16 17 18 19 20 21 22 23 24 25 26 27 28 29 30 31

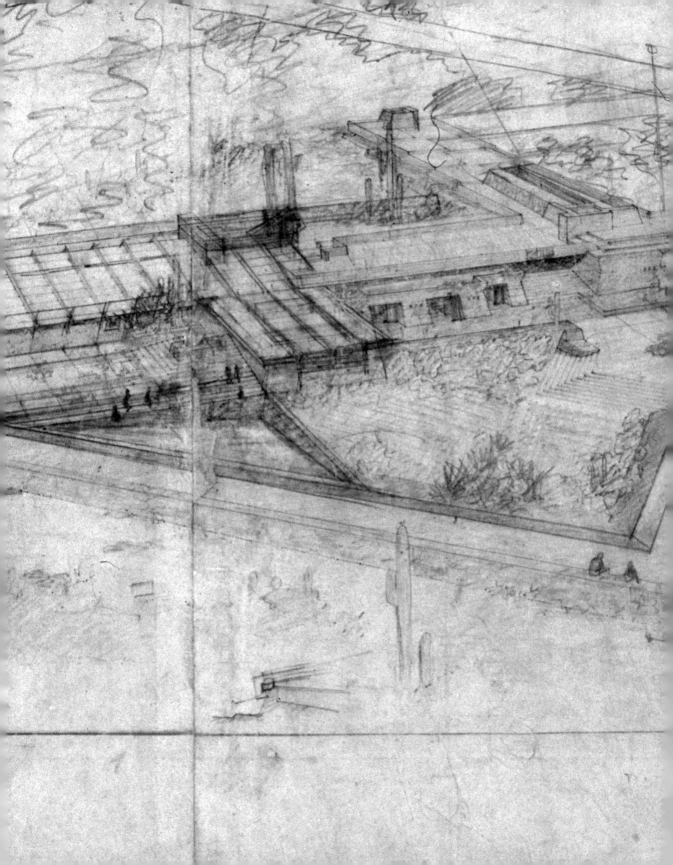

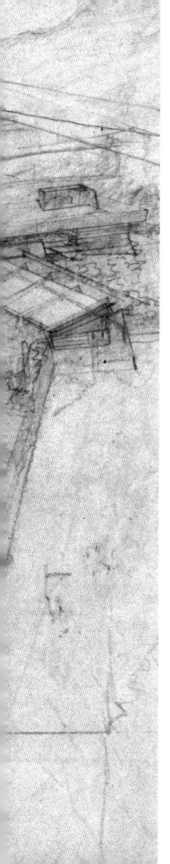

DECEMBER

○ 346 MONDAY

11

347 TUESDAY

12

348 WEDNESDAY

13

349 THURSDAY

14

350 FRIDAY

15

351 SATURDAY

16

352 SUNDAY

17

TALIESIN WEST (1937–59), SCOTTSDALE, ARIZONA. TALIESIN WEST'S TRIANGULAR PLAN AND MOTIFS ACKNOWLEDGE THE MOUNTAINS BEHIND IT.

DECEMBER

F	S	S	M	T	W	T	F	S	S	M	T	W	T	F	S	S	M	T	W	T	F	S	S	M	T	W	T	F	S	S
1	2	3	4	5	6	7	8	9	10	11	12	13	14	15	16	17	18	19	20	21	22	23	24	25	26	27	28	29	30	31

DECEMBER

MONDAY 353 ☽

18

TUESDAY 354

19

WEDNESDAY 355

20

THURSDAY 356

21

HANUKKAH (BEGINS AT SUNSET)
WINTER SOLSTICE 1:37 P.M. (GMT)

FRIDAY 357

22

SATURDAY 358

23

SUNDAY 359

24

TALIESIN WEST (1937–59), SCOTTSDALE, ARIZONA. A TRIANGULAR POOL BY THE DRAFTING ROOM FILLS THIS OASIS WITH REFRESHING WATER.

DECEMBER

F	S	S	M	T	W	T	F	S	S	M	T	W	T	F	S	S	M	T	W	T	F	S	S	M	T	W	T	F	S
1	2	3	4	5	6	7	8	9	10	11	12	13	14	15	16	17	18	19	20	21	22	23	24	25	26	27	28	29	30	31

DECEMBER

CHRISTMAS DAY ● 360 MONDAY
25

KWANZAA BEGINS □ BOXING DAY (CANADA AND UK) 361 TUESDAY
26

362 WEDNESDAY
27

363 THURSDAY
28

364 FRIDAY
29

365 SATURDAY
30

366 SUNDAY
31

TALIESIN WEST (1937–59), SCOTTSDALE, ARIZONA. WRIGHT CAME TO HIS DRAFTING ROOM EVEN IN 1959, WORKING RIGHT UP UNTIL HIS DEATH.

DECEMBER
F S S M T W T F S S M T W T F S S M T W T F S S M T W T F S S
1 2 3 4 5 6 7 8 9 10 11 12 13 14 15 16 17 18 19 20 21 22 23 24 25 26 27 28 29 30 31

2000

JANUARY

S	M	T	W	T	F	S
						1
2	3	4	5	6	7	8
9	10	11	12	13	14	15
16	17	18	19	20	21	22
23	24	25	26	27	28	29
30	31					

FEBRUARY

S	M	T	W	T	F	S
		1	2	3	4	5
6	7	8	9	10	11	12
13	14	15	16	17	18	19
20	21	22	23	24	25	26
27	28	29				

MARCH

S	M	T	W	T	F	S
			1	2	3	4
5	6	7	8	9	10	11
12	13	14	15	16	17	18
19	20	21	22	23	24	25
26	27	28	29	30	31	

APRIL

S	M	T	W	T	F	S
						1
2	3	4	5	6	7	8
9	10	11	12	13	14	15
16	17	18	19	20	21	22
23	24	25	26	27	28	29
30						

MAY

S	M	T	W	T	F	S
	1	2	3	4	5	6
7	8	9	10	11	12	13
14	15	16	17	18	19	20
21	22	23	24	25	26	27
28	29	30	31			

JUNE

S	M	T	W	T	F	S
				1	2	3
4	5	6	7	8	9	10
11	12	13	14	15	16	17
18	19	20	21	22	23	24
25	26	27	28	29	30	

JULY

S	M	T	W	T	F	S
						1
2	3	4	5	6	7	8
9	10	11	12	13	14	15
16	17	18	19	20	21	22
23	24	25	26	27	28	29
30	31					

AUGUST

S	M	T	W	T	F	S
		1	2	3	4	5
6	7	8	9	10	11	12
13	14	15	16	17	18	19
20	21	22	23	24	25	26
27	28	29	30	31		

SEPTEMBER

S	M	T	W	T	F	S
					1	2
3	4	5	6	7	8	9
10	11	12	13	14	15	16
17	18	19	20	21	22	23
24	25	26	27	28	29	30

OCTOBER

S	M	T	W	T	F	S
1	2	3	4	5	6	7
8	9	10	11	12	13	14
15	16	17	18	19	20	21
22	23	24	25	26	27	28
29	30	31				

NOVEMBER

S	M	T	W	T	F	S
			1	2	3	4
5	6	7	8	9	10	11
12	13	14	15	16	17	18
19	20	21	22	23	24	25
26	27	28	29	30		

DECEMBER

S	M	T	W	T	F	S
					1	2
3	4	5	6	7	8	9
10	11	12	13	14	15	16
17	18	19	20	21	22	23
24	25	26	27	28	29	30
31						

2001

JANUARY

S	M	T	W	T	F	S
	1	2	3	4	5	6
7	8	9	10	11	12	13
14	15	16	17	18	19	20
21	22	23	24	25	26	27
28	29	30	31			

FEBRUARY

S	M	T	W	T	F	S
				1	2	3
4	5	6	7	8	9	10
11	12	13	14	15	16	17
18	19	20	21	22	23	24
25	26	27	28			

MARCH

S	M	T	W	T	F	S
				1	2	3
4	5	6	7	8	9	10
11	12	13	14	15	16	17
18	19	20	21	22	23	24
25	26	27	28	29	30	31

APRIL

S	M	T	W	T	F	S
1	2	3	4	5	6	7
8	9	10	11	12	13	14
15	16	17	18	19	20	21
22	23	24	25	26	27	28
29	30					

MAY

S	M	T	W	T	F	S
		1	2	3	4	5
6	7	8	9	10	11	12
13	14	15	16	17	18	19
20	21	22	23	24	25	26
27	28	29	30	31		

JUNE

S	M	T	W	T	F	S
					1	2
3	4	5	6	7	8	9
10	11	12	13	14	15	16
17	18	19	20	21	22	23
24	25	26	27	28	29	30

JULY

S	M	T	W	T	F	S
1	2	3	4	5	6	7
8	9	10	11	12	13	14
15	16	17	18	19	20	21
22	23	24	25	26	27	28
29	30	31				

AUGUST

S	M	T	W	T	F	S
			1	2	3	4
5	6	7	8	9	10	11
12	13	14	15	16	17	18
19	20	21	22	23	24	25
26	27	28	29	30	31	

SEPTEMBER

S	M	T	W	T	F	S
						1
2	3	4	5	6	7	8
9	10	11	12	13	14	15
16	17	18	19	20	21	22
23	24	25	26	27	28	29
30						

OCTOBER

S	M	T	W	T	F	S
	1	2	3	4	5	6
7	8	9	10	11	12	13
14	15	16	17	18	19	20
21	22	23	24	25	26	27
28	29	30	31			

NOVEMBER

S	M	T	W	T	F	S
				1	2	3
4	5	6	7	8	9	10
11	12	13	14	15	16	17
18	19	20	21	22	23	24
25	26	27	28	29	30	

DECEMBER

S	M	T	W	T	F	S
						1
2	3	4	5	6	7	8
9	10	11	12	13	14	15
16	17	18	19	20	21	22
23	24	25	26	27	28	29
30	31					

Catalog No. 200008

ISBN 0-7649-0782-4

Published by Pomegranate Communications, Inc., Box 6099, Rohnert Park, California 94927
(800) 227-1428
www.pomegranate.com

Available in Canada from Firefly Books Ltd.
3680 Victoria Park Avenue, Willowdale, Ontario M2H 3K1

Available in the UK and mainland Europe from Pomegranate Europe Ltd.
Fullbridge House, Fullbridge, Maldon, Essex CM9 4LE, England

Available in Australia from Boobook Publications Pty Ltd.
P.O. Box 163 or Freepost 1, Tea Gardens 2324

Available in New Zealand from Randy Horwood Ltd.
P.O. Box 32-077, Devonport, Auckland

Available in Asia (including the Middle East), Africa, and Latin America
from Pomegranate International Sales
113 Babcombe Drive, Thornhill, Ontario L3T 1M9, Canada

Pomegranate also publishes the 2000 wall calendars *Frank Lloyd Wright's Designs for Living* and
Frank Lloyd Wright's Masterworks; the 2000 pocket calendar *Frank Lloyd Wright's Designs for Living;*
Frank Lloyd Wright® notecards, postcards, books of postcards, posters, magnets, bookmarks, and journals;
and the books *The House Beautiful,* the Wright at a Glance series, and *Frank Lloyd Wright's Fifty Views of Japan.*

Full-color catalogs of our calendars, notecards, notecard folios, boxed notes, postcards, books of postcards,
address books, books of days, posters, art magnets, Knowledge Cards™, bookmarks, journals,
and books are available for nominal fees. For more information on obtaining catalogs and ordering,
please write to Pomegranate, Box 6099, Rohnert Park, California 94927.

Solomon R. Guggenheim Museum. 1943–59. Pencil, color pencil, and ink on tracing paper. 26 × 39½". [4305.017]

Susan Lawrence Dana House. 1902–4. Four elevations. Ink on linen. 32 × 47". [9905.028]

Susan Lawrence Dana House. 1902–4. Dining room interior. Pencil and watercolor on paper. 23 × 19". [9905.003]

Susan Lawrence Dana House. 1902–4. Mural by George Niedecken. Ink and watercolor on paper. 11 × 16". [9905.033]

Susan Lawrence Dana House. 1902–4. Glass design. Pencil on tracing paper. 23 × 15". [9905.012]

Unitarian Meeting House. 1945–51. Perspective. Ink on tracing paper. 18 × 21". [5031.016]

Maximilian Hoffman House. 1955. Plan and rug design. Pencil and color pencil on tracing paper. 34 × 36". [5707.002]

Taliesin Fellowship Complex. 1932. Aerial perspective. Pencil and color pencil on tracing paper. 17¼ × 20½". [3301.001]

H. C. Price Company Tower. 1952–56. Perspective. Color pencil and ink on tracing paper. 48 × 34". [5215.003]

Press Building for the San Francisco Call (project). c.1913. Perspective. Ink and ink wash on linen. 38 × 17⅞". [1207.001]

John L. Rayward House. 1955. General plan. Color pencil and ink on tracing paper. 22 × 45". [5523.006]

Hillside Theater Curtain No. 2. 1952. Conceptual sketch. Pencil and color pencil on tracing paper. 21 × 38". [5223.001]

Beth Sholom Synagogue. 1953–59. Night view. Tempera on art board. 18⅛ × 29". [5313.142]

S. C. Johnson and Son, Inc., Administration Building. 1936–39. Interior perspective. Pencil and sepia ink on tracing paper. 11 × 34½". [3601.006]

Annunciation Greek Orthodox Church. 1955–61. Perspective. Color pencil and pencil on tracing paper. 19¾ × 52". [5611.002]

Taliesin West. 1937–59. Aerial perspective. Pencil, color pencil, and ink on tracing paper. 24 × 106". [3803.003]

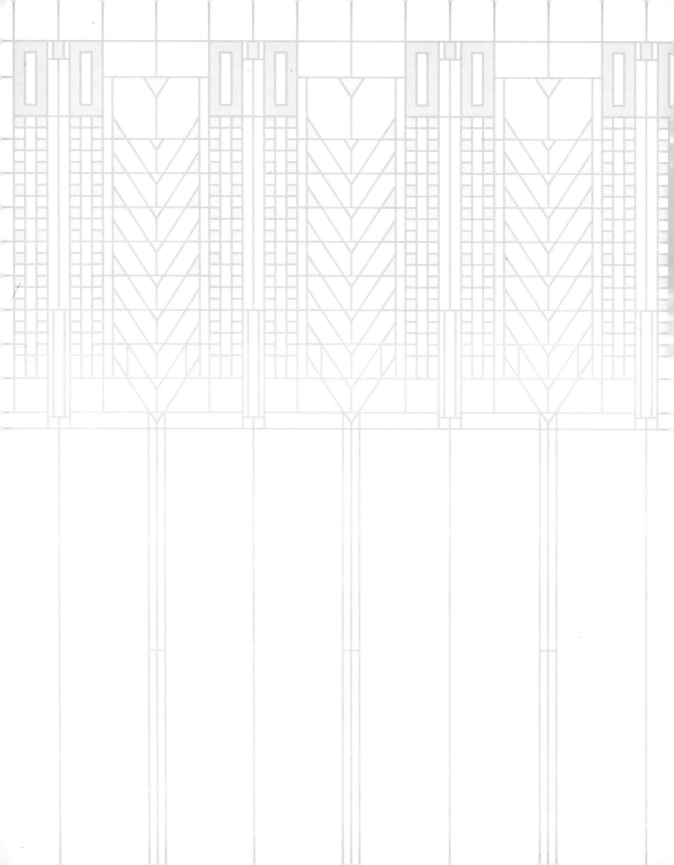